125 Motivators for Reading

Nicholas P. Criscuolo Ph.D.

Supervisor of Reading
New Haven Public Schools
New Haven, Connecticut

Fearon Teacher Aids
a division of
Pitman Learning, Inc.
Belmont, California

Copyright © 1977 by Pitman Learning, Inc., 6 Davis Drive, Belmont, California 94002. Member of the Pitman Group. All rights reserved. No part of this book may be reproduced by any means, transmitted, or translated into a machine language without written permission from the publisher.

ISBN-O-8224–5069-X

Library of Congress Catalog Card Number: 77-083523

Printed in the United States of America.

1.9876543

Edited by Carol L. King

Designed by Rick Chafian

Contents

Preface

"Reading is fun."

How many times have children heard it? Unfortunately, for too many youngsters in our schools, it's being heard, but they're not buying. Too many children do not like to read. Teachers must do everything we can to turn children back to reading, so that they will find it an enjoyable and satisfying experience.

This book has been prepared for that purpose. The activities in *125 Motivators for Reading* are classroom-tested and will serve to motivate children to want to read. With adaptations and modifications to accommodate different age levels, the activities can be used for children in all elementary grades.

When activities are fun-filled and creative, children will no longer say "I know how to read—but do I have to?" Rather, they will look forward to reading and readily sense all the joy it can offer.

Nicholas P. Criscuolo, Ph. D.
New Haven, Connecticut

I.

Choosing and Reviewing Books

Experience shows that children are more motivated to read books they have chosen themselves. Self-selection is a key concept in an individualized reading program because it gives children an opportunity to associate reading with pleasure. With so many children's books available today, there are stories to appeal to the special interests of every child. And yet the wide selection may be a drawback from the child's viewpoint. It is easy to imagine the confusion of a youngster who stands in the library, surrounded by hundreds of books, and wonders where to start browsing and how to narrow the choice down to one. It is crucial for teachers to provide a variety of activities designed to help students select the books they will enjoy.

Just as adults often read books recommended by their friends, children become interested in the books that their classmates talk about with enthusiasm. Although the old-fashioned book report still has value, there are many more imaginative ways to tell about books. The activities in this chapter enable children to tell others about the pleasure they have experienced from reading.

1 **Stick Puppets.**   Most children love puppets and tend to interact with them quite naturally. You can make simple stick puppets of the main characters from books.

If you have a damaged or outdated copy of the book, you can cut the characters out of the illustrations and paste them on popsicle sticks or tongue depressors.

A few days before the book is given to the students, introduce the puppets. Give each puppet's name and a few of his or her characteristics. Write the names on the board. When the children begin reading the book, they will know the characters as friends and should be able to read their names.

2 **Pick A Buddy.**   Ask children to pick a favorite book and then select a buddy. The buddies can read to each other in some quiet nook in the room.

3 **Prop Bag.**   Simple objects such as miniature cars, airplane models, dolls, and knitting needles, representing items mentioned in a popular book, can be placed in a prop bag by a student storyteller. As the student gives an oral review of a book, he/she reaches into the bag and uses the prop to enliven the presentation.

4 **File It.**   Provide a file box and a supply of 3 x 5 cards on which pupils may write their reactions to books they have read. Have the pupils decide what information they want to include on the cards and how they will arrange the file. The cards may be filed by author, title, or subject. In addition to including title, author, brief review, and the reviewer's signature on each card, pupils may want to tell whether the book can be obtained in the classroom, school library, or public library. Encourage pupils to write review cards frequently and to consult the cards when looking for something to read.

5 **How Do They Compare?**   Secure different editions of the same children's books, such as various Mother Goose books, *Alice in Wonderland, The Wizard of Oz,* and so on. Ask pupils to compare the illustrations. They can point out different styles and types of illustrations, such as fantasy versus realism, color versus black and white, or line drawings versus paintings or collage. Pupils may then tell which style they prefer for a particular book and why.

6 **It's in the News.**   Have pupils pretend that the events in a story or book really happened. Ask them to write an article that could be in a newspaper. They should tell the story as though it were a serious item of news. They might start with a headline like *Lion Walks the Streets* or *Cricket Visits Time Square.*

7 **Something Special.**   Each month have the school librarian print a list of all new materials in the library. Make two copies. Scan the list for items that would be of particular interest to the students. When a new book suits one of your students, write his or her name next to the title on the list. Give one copy to the librarian so the item will be reserved and use the other copy for yourself. Then tell each child on the list that you've reserved something special for him or her at the library. Children can then go to the library to locate the books.

8 **See Trees.**   Secure a tree branch and mount it in a coffee can containing sand. Using string, place several paperback books on the twigs of the branch.

This display will capture the interest of the children who can "pick" a book that looks appealing from the tree.

9 **Say It with Music.**   Music and reading can be combined to make book reports more effective. Ask a pupil to select a part of the book that conveys a mood, such as anger, serenity, or sorrow. The pupil can then select a record to play as an accompaniment as he or she reports this part of the book orally.

Segments of several records can also be put on a cassette tape and synchronized with a book report.

10 **Panel Discussions.** A group of students might present a panel discussion of the books they have read. It is not necessary for any two panel members to have read the same book.

Pupils can first discuss the problems faced by the major characters in stories. They can compare the stories they've read, and react to the kind of solution each story presents. Some guiding questions can be: (1) What was the major problem the main character faced? (2) How was the problem solved? (3) How would you have handled the problem? (4) How does this solution differ from the solutions mentioned by other members of the panel?

The class or panel may also discuss favorite characters, how they are alike or different, and why they like or do not like different ones.

11 **It's in the Headlines.** Making up "headlines" about books can be an interesting and stimulating activity. A headline such as "New Arrival Looks Like a Mouse" (*Stuart Little* written by E. B. White and published by Harper & Row) might be posted on the bulletin board and children encouraged to guess which book is represented. After a few experiences with these headlines, many of your pupils will enjoy making their own headlines as riddles for the class.

12 **Classroom Museum.**   Explore with the group the possibility of bringing in some interesting objects discussed in the books they have been reading. Such objects as a serape, chopsticks, an Indian headdress, and Mexican pottery will serve to enrich reading. Set up a little museum to house these objects in the classroom. Other classes might be invited to visit this museum.

Be sure to tag the object with a slip of paper stating the title and author of the book in which the object is mentioned.

13 **Chart It.**   Encourage readers to read in many different fields by keeping a record of material read independently. Pupils can prepare charts divided into such categories as adventure, travel, poetry, and biographies. Each time a pupil reads a book in a particular field, he or she colors in the appropriate section. This is a good technique because it encourages readers to explore a wide variety of subjects.

14 **Preparing Lists.**   Urge children to bring their library books to school and share them with the other class members. As a group project, the children might prepare a list of favorite books as suggestions to parents for home purchase.

This activity could be extended by having the children prepare Christmas lists and summer reading lists of their favorite books. Send the lists home to parents before the Christmas and summer vacation periods.

15 **Quiz Shows.** Quiz shows patterned after "What's My Line?" or "Twenty Questions" offer an opportunity for pupils who have read certain books to become well acquainted with their favorite characters in those books. A pupil pretends to be a certain character. The class—or a representative group—tries to determine who the character is by asking questions, to which the "character" may answer only yes or no.

16 **Fishbowl Fun.** Fill a fishbowl with short statements or interesting questions from books. Include the author's name and the title of the book. Fasten a paper clip to each card. At the end of a pencil place a string to which a magnet is attached. Ask children to "fish" for the statements. After reading the statement or question, children may be stimulated to read the actual book.

17 **Skim the Books.** Ask each pupil to choose from the class or school library a fiction book that he/she especially enjoyed during the school year. Ask the children to skim the books quickly in order to find the best parts. The selections should consist of several paragraphs from various parts of the book, but should not reveal the ending. Have the children reread their choices silently, and then set a time for them to read the selections aloud to the class or group.

18 **Sales Pitch.** Instead of the usual written or oral book report, try having pupils "sell" the books they have read to the class. It's the job of the reader to convince the class that his/her product (book) is the best book of its kind. If you find two pupils who have read books on the same topic or theme, let them both "sell" their books. Pupils can compare the different sales pitches for effectiveness.

19 **Birthday Gift.** As part of the birthday celebration for a pupil in your room, let the birthday child pick his favorite story from those you have read to the class. Read it to the class at an appropriate time during the day.

20 **Book Auction.** First, select an auctioneer and choose a recorder to catalog the seller, buyer, title, and price of the books and the date of the auction. Then ask each child to select a book to "sell."

Using tokens or play money, give each pupil fifty points (using five- and ten-point denominations). Additional points can be obtained only by selling a book. All points are collected at the end of the auction.

Give a child sixty seconds to "sell" a book. He/she should have read all or most of the book. Encourage the child to say just enough to whet the appetite of the audience.

Pupils then bid for books until a high bidder is determined. (Pupils may use their fifty points and any other points obtained from selling books.) In case of ties, the auctioneer decides who gets the book.

21 **Line It Up.**   Ask each child to select a character or important object from a book. The child should draw a picture of it, cut the picture out, and trace the outline of the picture on a piece of lined paper. Then the pupil should cut the lined paper along the picture outline.

Direct the children to write summaries of their books on the lined papers, then staple the drawing and the summary together.

22 **Send a Telegram.**   Show the class some telegrams or telegram facsimiles. Then ask each child to write an exciting telegram about the main idea of a book. For added interest, allow the children to make telegrams by cutting the words from a magazine and pasting them on paper. Post the telegrams on the class bulletin board.

23 **Character Clues.**   As the children read their basic reading text or a collection of story books, ask them to develop a list of statements (clues) about each important character. Use the lists for a guessing game. See how many clues must be given before the group can guess who the character is.

For a continuing activity of this type, have the children write questions and place them in envelope pockets on the bulletin board. One envelope labeled "Who am I?" might contain clue-questions about characters, such as "I'm a monkey who took a trip around the world. Who am I?" Another envelope labeled "Where did it happen?" might include questions about events; for example, "A mean man found a large package. Where did it happen?"

When the children have read the entire text, or a number of trade books, the questions in the envelopes can be used to refresh fond memories of books and stories.

24

Danger Problem Cards. Describe the danger or problem faced by the main character in a particular book. For example:

Book: "The Hidden Cave"

Author: Jaime Swan

Main Character: Lisa Tripp

Lisa was excited as she explored the cave. It was dark inside the cave but she had a flashlight. She shouted to the walls and they answered back.

Just then she heard a cracking noise behind her. She turned around quickly and saw a man with a long, white beard.

What did Lisa do?

Ask the children to decide what they would have done in the situation described. As a final step, have the children check the book to find out what the character did.

25

Reviewer's Corner. Reviewing books in small groups offers a pleasant change from giving book reviews to the entire class. Divide your class into three or four groups and let each group meet in one corner of the room. Encourage the pupils to ask questions and exchange information about each book reviewed. You may wish to set a time limit for each book review so that each child will have an opportunity to participate as a reviewer.

26 **Lost and Found.** Have the students make up "Lost and Found" ads for persons or objects in books. On the back of each ad, the child should write his or her own name, the title of the book, and the name of the author. For example:

LOST Anyone finding a large green ring in the Oaklawn section of town, please return to Sandy. Call 462-0175. Reward.	*Book:* "The Green Ring" *Author:* John Cable *Placer of Ad:* Billy Jones

These ads can be placed on the classroom bulletin board. As the children read various books, they respond to the ads by guessing the names of books and authors.

Two prizes can be awarded for this activity. One prize is for the first pupil to guess a designated number of books through these ads. To award another prize, let the children vote to decide which member of the class contributed the best ads.

27 **Map-O-Rama.** Use a large map and pieces of yarn to locate countries, cities, or towns where the action of various stories takes place. Each piece of yarn can be extended from the designated spot to a file card on which a child has written a summary of major events in a book or story. This display can be used for a unit of stories in a basal reader or for a group of trade books read by the entire class.

28 **Computerized Dating.** The child has a date with a book! Before the date is set, ask each child to fill out the date application below.

Name _____ Age _____

Hobbies _____

Favorite TV Program _____

Last Book I Read _____

Types of Books I like _____

This information will show what kinds of books children in the class would enjoy reading. The teacher serves as the "computer" by checking the school or class library to match the child with an appropriate book, based on information gleaned from the completed applications.

29 **Puzzle It Out.** Use large pieces of white cardboard. On each piece, write the title of a book in crayon. Write some of the main ideas from the book in the form of plot "teasers" to arouse the children's curiosity. Cut the cardboard into fairly large pieces of different shapes. These pieces will constitute a puzzle.

As children put the puzzles together, they may be motivated to read the books that capture their interest.

30 **Situation Wanted.** Ask students to write a job wanted ad for the main character in the book. To do this, they'll have to consider the character carefully, and decide what kind of situation he/she would want to be involved in. Example:

> SITUATION WANTED
>
> I am looking for an exciting, well-paying job. Danger is my business. Not afraid to take chances. Will keep every confidence. If interested, call 627-9432 after 8 p.m. Ask for "X".

These ads can be posted on the bulletin board to serve as the basis for guessing books and characters.

31 **TV Re-runs.** Television shows such as "I've Got a Secret" and "This Is Your Life" can be imitated in the classroom in order to motivate children to read.

For the "I've Got a Secret" game, each child pretends that he/she is either the character or the author of a particular book. The secret is one of the events in the story. A panel of children who have read the book try to guess the secret by asking questions that can be answered yes or no.

For "This Is Your Life," one student plays the role of the surprised guest, a character from one of the books the children have read. Other students appear to recall events that happened to this character in the story.

32   **Rate It.**   Teach children to evaluate the books and stories they read critically. Discuss a rating scale: 1—Excellent, 2—Good, 3—Fair, 4—Poor. Explain that a book can be judged on the basis of these points: interesting plot or story line, attractive illustrations, interesting writing style, and good character development. The children may be allowed to suggest additional points for evaluation. Each child may wish to compile the following chart as part of the reporting system:

Date	Title	Character(s) Involved	The Problem Situation	The Outcome	Your Rating
Feb. 6	"Laura's Discovery"	Laura Conductor Mr. Lee	Laura finds a large sum of money on a train.	She decides to try to locate owner.	2

2.

Using Arts and Crafts

Although reading tends to be a passive activity, the motivation to read and the activities that result from reading do not have to be passive. Participation in a total reading experience can be both active and energizing.

The use of arts and crafts has special appeal for children. These activities involve the learner, add an extra dimension to reading, and allow for the integration of reading with other subject areas, such as art and music. The products that result from arts and crafts activities are tangible evidence that reading has not only taken place but has proved to be an enjoyable experience as well.

33

Meet the Pals. Inspire interest in reading with "Reading Pals," stuffed toy companions that sit in a child's lap or on the floor and "listen" while the child reads.

To make a Reading Pal, each student will need two large pieces of heavy white cloth, crayons, scissors, a large blunt needle, yarn, and stuffing material, such as cotton or shredded newspaper.

Have each student fold one piece of heavy cloth lengthwise and draw half an animal or person on one side of the fold, making sure that the body is on the fold with arms and legs extending out. (In the lower grades, the teacher may wish to provide a cardboard pattern.) With the cloth still folded, the pupil should cut along the outline. This first shape can then be used as a pattern to draw an identical figure on the second piece of cloth. The child should cut out the second figure also.

Each student should draw a face on one of the two cloth figures. The child may wish to add other details, such as stripes or spots on animals.

The student can then sew the two figures together, using small stitches about one-half inch from the edge of the cutout, but leaving a small opening through which the stuffing can be inserted. This opening should be sewed after the figure has been stuffed.

Encourage the youngsters to read aloud to their Pals during free time in class or at home.

34

Coat Hanger Book Reports. Ask children to draw a picture depicting a major scene from a book and paste these pictures on construction paper the width of a wire coat hanger. Make paper rings so that each sheet can be hung on the cross piece of a hanger.

Have the children write the name of the book and its author on the back of the picture. These attractive coat hanger book reports can then be hung about the room.

35

Mounted Scenes. From plaster of paris mounted on plywood, have pupils construct a scene from one of their favorite books, for example, a scene from *Treasure Island*. Colored construction paper can be used to make tiny birds and lush plants to enhance the scene.

A paragraph or two can be written on a file card to explain the scene. This card can be attached to the edge of the plywood.

36

Post the Posters. Ask children to make a poster by drawing a picture from a favorite book on a large piece of white paper. Have them write the title and author of the book in dark letters below the picture. Hang these posters on the wall or bulletin board.

37

Book Friends. Ask children to draw pictures of some of their favorite storybook characters. After the pictures have been drawn and colored, the children can cut them out. They can then tie a string onto each cutout and tie the other end of the string to a hanger. These pictures are now part of a mobile, which can be hung in the classroom in an appropriate location. These story characters almost come to life for the children!

Related to this activity, children can make small paper masks for each of these story characters. The masks will form an appealing bulletin board display and also serve as a reminder that children can meet many good friends in books.

38 **Map It Out.** Provide copies of American folk songs for pupils to read. Then sing the songs with the children or play recordings of the songs.

Choose folk songs that truly represent different parts of the United States. Then ask pupils to color a large map of the United States to show the region with which each song is associated. Display the finished map on a bulletin board or in a strategic place in the classroom.

39 **What's Ahead.** Discover individual pupil interests early in the year. Distribute reading books and supply textbooks. Invite the students to leaf through them. Then have them make a pair of construction paper or crayon eyes (paper eyelashes curled around a pencil add much) at the top of a sheet of paper with "Looking Ahead" printed under the eyes.

Let them draw pictures at the bottom of their papers of something they saw that especially interested them. A short commentary can be written by the child to accompany the picture. These pictures will help you to recommend appropriate books for independent reading.

40 **Wanted.** Have each child make a "Wanted" poster for someone he or she is interested in—a fictional or historical figure or a contemporary personality.

Children will need pictures of themselves as the characters. These can be taken in class or brought from home.

When the students write their individual posters, they should take some liberties with what the crime is. For example, Mary Poppins might be wanted for flying without a license.

These posters make an attractive wall display.

41 **Cartoon Capers.** Encourage students to use their sense of humor by creating cartoons for the bulletin board. They'll need white construction paper and felt pens.

Students can glean ideas from song titles, TV programs, newspaper and magazine ads, and so on. For example, try these:

"Don't Fence Me In"

"Try It, You'll Like It!"

"I Ate the Whole Thing!"

"Fly Me to the Moon!"

"Everybody Wants a Piece of the Action"

"Pie in the Sky!"

42 **Stage Settings.** Books consist of various settings and locales. Pupils can construct a miniature stage setting for part of a book or the entire book, perhaps from a cardboard or wooden box. Discarded materials and all sorts of odds and ends can be used for background and props. Small dolls of various kinds (cardboard, wire, pipe cleaner, paperdolls) can be used. Small toys of various kinds can serve as props.

Pupils can attach a 5 x 7 file card to the stage, identifying the book and telling what occurred in this setting.

43 **Shadow Panels.** To add dramatic effect for pupils telling a story to the class or narrating a play, ask students to make "shadow panels." Have them cut silhouettes of characters and scenes from colored construction paper. These silhouettes can be mounted on a sheet of white tissue paper, and covered with another sheet of white tissue. As pupils tell the story, they can show a shadow panel for each scene, holding it up against the light so that the silhouettes stand out.

44 **Accordion Story Book.**   Have each child in the class make an accordion storybook by cutting oaktag into long strips. Fold each strip into even sections and ask pupils to draw on it a major scene from a book recently read. As the child orally recounts the major action of the story, he or she can "play" the accordion.

45 **Collage Posters.**   Add a creative spark to reading by making attractive collage posters. Ask each student to select a recently read book and to make a list of main ideas, characters, and other important elements.

Bring in a supply of old magazines. The children can cut out letters, words, phrases, pictures, or parts of pictures that illustrate or spell out the items on their lists.

Next ask each student to select a piece of bright-colored construction paper, arrange the cutouts on it, and paste them into position. Remind the students to include the title and author's name.

46 **Design a Bookmark.**   Have children design a bookmark for a favorite book. The design can contain a saying from the book or an illustration of a character or event found interesting. These bookmarks can be given as gifts.

47 **Shape It, Scrape It, or Drape It.** A variety of media and materials can be used to report on reading done. Pupils can do a soap or balsa wood carving of a scene or character. They can make stand-up characters or puppets and design costumes for them. They can make a collage or construct a wire mobile or build a scale model of an important object in the book.

48 **Puppet Power.** Have your pupils make hand puppets of favorite story characters. The puppets may be made from paper bags or cloth scraps. Have the pupils tell about the story and act it out using the puppets they have made.

49 **Rebus Reading.** In a rebus, pictures are substituted for nouns throughout a sentence or paragraph. Ask each child to create a rebus story to match a book that he/she has read. Have the student write or print the story on lined paper and paste in small pictures cut from magazines or catalogs.

Some students might enjoy collecting a rebus reservoir by clipping pictures that look usable—objects, people, and animals—and placing them in a set of labeled envelopes for future rebus-writing sessions.

50

Reading Mobilizers. Engage students in a simple mobile-making project that adds swing to book reporting and at the same time offers the children practice in culling significant information from their reading.

Suggest that each student make a list of important quotes, characters, words, and incidents from a recently read book. Explain that these will become part of the mobile.

Each student will need index cards, thread, tape, scissors, and a wire hanger. The students should cut the cards into different shapes. They might choose rectangles or squares for quotes, a profile or a body shape for characters, and so on. These items can be hung on thread from the wire hanger, either side by side or one below the other. Have the children cut the thread into different lengths and decide upon a vertical sequence for their cutouts.

These mobiles can be hung from heavy string tied across the front or back of the classroom.

51

Collage Reports. Have students cut out magazine or newspaper pictures that depict an idea, theme, or scene from a book they have read. The pictures should be pasted onto a backing sheet of construction paper or oaktag. Around the pictures, let students arrange words or phrases that explain, describe, or represent the story. Have them also look for adjectives and vivid verbs. On the lower back corner of the backing sheet have students attach an index card, briefly recounting the book's theme, plot, author, and publisher.

52 **Pic-a-Vision.** Favorite TV programs can be depicted on construction paper television sets. Discuss the programs first, and then suggest to the children that they illustrate their favorite shows.

Children can look through magazines, cut out pictures, and paste them on their drawn TV "screens."

Ask children to then locate books related to these television programs. For instance, *Robin Hood* and books on science fiction would be related to Space 1999.

53 **Fill the Vase.** Have children draw a vase from construction paper and paste it on oaktag. Tell children that every time they read a book they can cut a paper flower, write the title of the book and the name of its author on its petals, and paste it in the vase. It will be fun for the children to fill up their vases.

3.

Reading Games and Creative Writing

For the child who is learning to read, reading is "work." One way to show children that "reading can be fun" is to associate reading with play. Games make reading active, rather than passive. They add the satisfaction of interacting with others to the solitary activity of reading. Whether it is searching newspapers for important ideas or hunting a "treasure" by following written clues, children will respond more eagerly when the element of play is involved. Games motivate and increase involvement as they help students to glean new insights and information from reading.

Creative writing helps children to consolidate their insights and information. It gives them a chance to share their experience. Writing can be fun too, when the emphasis is upon sharing, imagination, and spontaneous self-expression. By sharing, children will learn to think of writing as a good way to communicate and to elicit response from others.

54   **Buy It—You'll Like It!**   Ask children to select a book they liked reading very much. Then have them write a business letter to a librarian stating reasons why the book should be purchased.

55   **Next-Door Neighbor.**   Many children readily identify with story characters. Ask children who have recently completed a book to identify its main character and then write a few paragraphs on why they would like or dislike living next-door to the character in the book.

56   **Sequels.**   Ask pupils to read a particular story or book and tell them that they can write a sequel to it. For instance, they can write about the continued journey of a spacecraft or the further adventures of a major character.

57   **Unusual Place Names.**   Some towns in the United States have unusual and interesting names. Ask pupils if they have ever visited Hot Coffee, Mississippi, Polka Dot, Ohio, Double Trouble, New Jersey, or Last Chance, Colorado.

Motivate students to learn more about these places by writing to the Chamber of Commerce for descriptive literature revealing how they got their names. Material received will make interesting reading!

58 **Class Documentary.** In the fall, take several rolls of film, showing the children in typical school activities, including gym, art, music, and lunch. Compile the pictures in a photo album and let each child write sentences to accompany the pictures.

Additional scrapbooks of class activities can be compiled using a camera. This collection can be shown to parents, to give them a clear picture of what their child has been doing.

59 **Getting to Know You.** At the beginning of the year, make up a free-verse poem about all the things you like. Kids like to know what kind of person their teacher is. Then ask students to write a poem about things they like so that everyone can become better acquainted. After the poems have been shared, the students make collages of the things they like. These become the covers for their creative book reports done during the year.

60 **Send a Note.** A pupil who has read and enjoyed a book can suggest that book to a peer. Reserve a space on the bulletin board for notes from one pupil to another. For example:

Dear Jose:

I just finished reading "Call Me Charlie." It's about a boy and his friend. Lots of things happen to them. You can get a copy of it at the Reading Corner. Try it, you'll like it.

Your friend,
Pete

61 **Magazine Mileage.**   Use old children's magazines for free reading. Tear them apart and staple the stories in folders. Color code them according to difficulty. If desired, add comprehension questions or cut off the ending to allow children to write their own endings.

62 **Another Time, Another Place.**   Have children write stories about different phases of their lives as they might have happened had they lived in another time and place. "Important Happenings During My Life," "Important People in My Life," "My Library (Kinds of Books I Like and Why)," or "The Most Exciting Thing That Ever Happened to Me" might be some choices. Combine the stories into a book entitled "My Autobiography," which can be shown to parents and classmates.

63 **Texture Poems.**   Ask the children to use their tactile sense by picking an object, such as a piece of fur, a stuffed animal, a piece of sandpaper. Have them classify the object as being smooth, furry, wrinkled, or rough. Lists can be compiled of things that are smooth, furry, wrinkled, and rough.

Each child can then select one texture category and one of the words listed under that category. From this central idea he/she can compose a poem. These poems can be duplicated and shared with the rest of the class.

64 **Mood Poetry.** Display photographs of people's faces, cut from magazines or newspapers. The pictures should be interesting and should convey a mood or feeling. Ask the children to choose one that they particularly like and tell them to write a poem about it with a mood theme.

Include some of the poems and pictures in a class anthology.

65 **Classroom Storybook.** A classroom storybook encourages children to write their own stories. (For ideas, keep a picture file box with magazine pictures brought in by the children.) When a story has been written, it is placed in a manila folder. Type the story. Have the "author" illustrate it and place it in the class storybook. Children may take the book home to read to their families.

66 **Mail-a-Book.** Have children create their own stories. Below each story the "author" must write his or her name. Designate someone to pick up each day's "mail." This mail, which consists of the stories written by the children, can then be typed by you or an aide and returned to the child. The child can then illustrate each story and make a cover for his/her book of stories.

These "books" can then be placed in the Reading Center for supplementary reading.

67   **Book of Rhymes.** Ask children to make up a book of question rhymes as a class project. These rhymes should be illustrated. As starters ask the children to illustrate the following rhymes:

>   Did you ever see a dish fish?
>
>   Did you ever see a ring swing?
>
>   Did you ever see a paper clip flip?
>
>   Did you ever see a book look?
>
>   Did you ever see a map clap?

Rhymes can be compiled in a book and placed in the Reading Corner for extra reading.

68   **Classified Ads.** Have children make up classified ads and read them to each other. Suggest making the ads funny or mysterious. You might also suggest writing a "Lost" or "Found" ad for an item lost in a story, such as Cinderella's glass slipper. Here are some examples:

>   *For Sale*: Wedding Veil. Never worn. Reasonable price. Call 326-3491 as soon as possible.
>
>   *Wanted*: Anyone who saw two men loading a truck last Monday night near Elm and Grand, call 283-4061. Handsome reward.
>
>   *Found*: One blue shoe at corner of Fox and Evergreen Streets. Must prove ownership by trying on shoe. Call Ms. Carter, at 329-8764.

69   **Feelings Unlimited.** Have a Feelings Unlimited box in your room. Students are told that they can write a short paragraph about how a character felt at a critical moment in a story recently read. The paragraph can be written on a file card with the child's name on the back. Writers can supply as many clues as they wish but must omit the character's name and the title of the book. Other students try to identify the book or story on the basis of these clues.

70   **Look It Up!** Prepare some questions that need to be researched and ask your students to go to the school library to look up the answers. Type the questions on individual file cards and ask each student to draw three cards at random. To add zest to the activity, give the students a specified period of time to find the answers. Perhaps a prize could be awarded to the first youngster who completes the assignment correctly. (So that answers can be verified, instruct the children to write down the source of each answer.)

Use these questions as starters:

- Who holds the world's record for catching the largest shark?
- Is Rio de Janeiro north or south of Buenos Aires?
- What was the score of the 1962 Cotton Bowl football game?
- What is the present population of China?
- How tall is the Washington Monument?

71

Cartoon Fun.   Use comic strips to add some zest to the reading program. Select some cartoons such as "Peanuts," "Beetle Bailey," and "Dennis the Menace." Have students cut out each sequence, number the segments on the reverse side, then shuffle the pictures from their original order. Clip together each sequence with the title of the strip attached. Have children put them in order.

Have children also prepare book reports in the form of cartoons.

72

Journalistic Pen Pals.   To encourage children to write with a purpose, begin a pen-pal program with a high school journalism class. Enlist the aid of the high school class and its teacher so that your goals will be clearly understood. Each child should have a pen pal in the journalism class. The journalism students may be willing to assign topics for your children to write about (or news stories to "cover") in order to stimulate creativity. They might also send the high school newspaper, which will give your students great pleasure—especially when they see their pen pals' by-lines. Your students will eagerly await the day the "mailbag" comes.

73

Clipping Service.   Ask students to bring current newspapers and news magazines to class. These periodicals provide an excellent source for large pictures and articles on leaders and events important in world affairs. Have the students clip these articles. Provide a clipping file, which can be used as a stimulus for further reading about these topics.

74

It's in the Phone Book!   Here is a way to use old phone books in your classroom to spark reading. Type each task on a separate index card, and let each child choose a card at random. Have the children put their finished papers in a scrapbook.

- List people whose last names are colors. (Example: Mary Brown)
- List people whose last names are the same as girls' names. (Henry Janet)
- List people whose last names are the same as boys' names. (Tina Mark)
- List people whose last names are things to eat. (Joe Apple)
- List people whose last names are occupations. (Nick Carpenter)
- List people with the same names as famous people. (Jimmy Carter)
- List people whose last names are compound words. (Jerry Wintergreen)

75

Treasure Hunt.   Provide items such as models or inexpensive games to serve as treasures. Write clues on 3 × 5 file cards, and number the cards so that the child can follow the directions in order. Card 1 might read, "Go to the teacher's desk. Look under the blotter." Under the blotter is card 2, and so on.

76

What's the Code?   Write the titles of books in code form. Give the students one example of a coded book title and illustrate how to decode it. Then ask each child to figure out the correct title of a book, read it, and write a short summary of it in code. Thus, the children can try to figure out the code and become familiar with the book at the same time.

77   **Forum on Issues.**   Have each pupil select a local issue, such as pollution, nuclear wastes, or crime control, and read up on the issue selected. Schedule an "Issues Forum" at which all the children who have chosen a particular topic will take part in a round-table discussion on that issue.

Help the children to gather resource material on their issues from newspapers and magazines or by contacting local citizens groups for pertinent information.

78   **It's in My Diary.**   Ask your pupils to write a diary or "log" representing the experiences of the main character in a book. Each child can pretend to be this character, recording events as they happen. Show the children a diary so that they will understand the division of entries by years, months, and dates.

79   **Birthday Calendars.**   Read the poems of such famous poets as Robert Frost, Emily Dickinson, and Alfred Noyes to the class. Then, as a class or group project, have the children list their favorite poets. Have them look up the birthday of each poet in the classroom or school library and prepare calendars noting these birthdays.

The children can then be encouraged to compile a selection of poems to read on the birthday of each poet.

80 **Storybook House.** A place of honor should be available for the many stories and papers written by the children. A story house can be constructed from large boxes and cartons. (Perhaps you can find an appliance dealer who is willing to contribute the boxes in which large appliances, such as refrigerators and washing machines, are shipped.) The teacher and students construct and paint the house together, adding new details according to the number of stories and papers written by the children. For example, two stories can earn a window. A "cost list" can be developed mutually by both teacher and class.

When the house is completed, each child can be given an area of the roof on which to display his/her collection.

In free time, the children will love to kick off their shoes, curl up in a corner of the carpeted house, and quietly read a book or write a story.

81 **Sleuthing with Newspapers.** Children enjoy sleuthing. Use certain sections of yesterday's daily newspaper for this activity. Have a committee of students prepare a set of questions to be duplicated and handed out to the other students. They must skim the newspapers to find the answers. The class learns to read headlines carefully and then skims through paragraphs for definite information. It's fun and builds skills too.

82 **Reference Preference.** Have each pupil consult a reference book of quotations. Make a collection of famous quotations that describe ideas or feelings about (a) evildoers; (b) well-known historical figures; (c) foolishness or folly; (d) sadness; (e) happiness, and so on.

Have the children share their quotations. Select a favorite for each category.

83 **Read-Around-the-Room.** Ask each child to select a brief story to be read aloud. Hold a drawing to decide who starts the "Read-Around." The winner (Child A) is allowed to choose the first story and select a classmate (Child B) to read it aloud. After reading the story to the class, Child B sends his or her favorite story to another classmate, Child C, who reads it aloud. Encourage the children to keep on going around the room until everyone has had a chance to read to the class.

84 **Poems for Four Seasons.** Seasonal poetry evokes meaningful images. Have youngsters compile favorite poems about the four seasons. Children can scour anthologies, books of poetry, and other sources to locate these seasonal poems. For example:

> The morns are meeker than they were,
> The nuts are getting brown;
> The berry's cheek is plumper,
> The rose is out of town.
>
> The maple wears a gayer scarf,
> The field a scarlet gown;
> Lest I should be old-fashioned,
> I'll put a trinket on.
>
> *Emily Dickinson*

Ask the children to read the poems of such writers as Robert Frost, Sara Teasdale, Rachel Field, and Walter de la Mare to locate other seasonal poetry. The following sourcebooks will prove helpful:

Arbuthnot, May Hill. *Time for Poetry.* Scott, Foresman, 1968.

O'Neill, Mary. *Hailstones and Halibut Bones.* Doubleday, 1961.

4.

Class Projects

Although reading is usually a solitary activity, projects that require reading can be assigned as team endeavors. They may even involve an entire class.

Reading takes place each and every day. You can demonstrate this concept effectively by engaging children in events that require an extended period of time for preparation and presentation of materials. The extended time period gives the children experience in planning for future events and develops their capacity to integrate groups of ideas and impressions derived from their reading.

Some of the activities in this chapter are continuing projects that can be extended over the entire school year. Projects such as compiling a class book draw children to the "Reading Corner," sustain interest, and serve as motivators for reading.

85   **Dress-up-Day.** Have a "Dress-up" day. Ask pupils to select a character from a book recently read. Tell students to dress as that person and tell what role he/she plays in the story.

It is interesting to have children prepare a dialogue between two book characters drawn from different eras. In the dialogue, some useful information can be imparted related to a specific time period.

86   **The Talking Mural.** Have pupils make a "talking mural." The mural can be constructed from oaktag pasted onto heavy cardboard. They can paint a series of pictures keynoting important events from a particular book. Students can cut out holes for the faces to look through, thus they become part of the picture as they dramatize or discuss an event from the book.

87   **Happy Birthday.** Have pupils make birthday cards for relatives or friends who are having birthdays soon. The children as a group can make up a birthday verse. Print the verse on a large sheet of paper and post it in the classroom.

88 **Sound Off about Books.** Liven up book reports by introducing oral alternatives.

Pupils can sing a report to the tune of a well-known song from radio, record, TV, or other source. Children with developed musical skills can work alone or in teams to compose a simple tune with lyrics based on a book.

Ask students to make a book character doll and serve as ventriloquist, while the doll relates highlights from the story. (The doll used in this activity can be a ready-made doll dressed in an appropriate costume.)

89 **Ready Resources.** Every community has resource people who can be asked to share their talents and experiences. Make a list of topics that will be read about in class in the future. Topics particularly appropriate for this activity are those that deal with travel. For example, people in the community who have visited foreign countries can be invited to the class to show slides and artifacts and discuss their experiences, so that as children read stories that take place in these countries, the characters and scenes will come alive for them.

Prior to such a visit, members of the class can interview these resource people, and write a brief report as well as an introduction for the visitor.

90 **Fun Box.** To help children develop their sense of humor and to recognize absurdities, start a Fun Box in your room. Select jokes, puns, limericks, and cartoons from children's magazines and newspapers and make up your own absurdities. Write or type them on small slips of paper and put them in the Fun Box.

Decorate the box with pictures of clowns, jesters, well-known comedians, or absurd situations.

91 **Important Notice Board.** Put up an Important Notice Board in your room. This board can contain notices of assemblies, field trips, and other important events. Keep the information concise: Where, When, Who, What. It can also be used by the children to notify their classmates that at a specified time (usually Sharing Period) they will be reading a limerick, rhyme, or poem, or that they will be giving a brief report on a "fantastic" book just read.

92 **Scrapbook Friends.** Suggest to the group that they begin now to make a scrapbook about the story characters they've been reading about. Let pupils help you select a title for the book. One possible title is "Friends We've Met." Explain that from time to time they will need to draw pictures of story characters and paste them in the book.

93 **Poetry Club.** Children who find poems they like particularly well are eligible to join the Poetry Club. To become a member, a child must write the poem in an individual booklet, illustrate it, and save it for Poetry Club.

When the day for Poetry Club arrives, all who have poems to share can read them to the class, and show the illustrations made to accompany the poems selected.

94 Who's Who. Have each child write his/her full name and address on a large loose-leaf notebook page. List hobbies, personal information, and the types of books he or she enjoys reading. Put the pages in the notebook, in alphabetical order.

Children in the class can use the book for reference in sending holiday greetings or get-well letters. Encourage children to list the titles of a few books they think the recipient would enjoy, based on the biographical data supplied.

95 Read-Along. Ask students to make a tape recording of a short book they have read. A few follow-up questions might be asked related to specific events in the story. Later other students in the class can read along with the tape and answer the questions.

This is an excellent activity to share with other children in the school — particularly children in the primary grades.

96 Spring Planting. Have students bring in some old seed catalogs. Ask them to find pictures and descriptions of various plants, information on planting times, and planting directions.

Students can read these catalogs to plan a class spring indoor garden or prepare a handbook for spring walks. Students will be pleased that, after reading these catalogs, they will be able to identify the different kinds of plants on their walks or visits to community gardens.

97   **Armchair Travelers.** If children have read a travel book, they can present an illustrated lecture using postcards, photographs, slides, and pictures clipped from magazines.

As a backdrop, a large poster of a particular country can be used to add flavor to the presentation.

The children can also read travel books to plan a round-the-world cruise.

98   **Class Journalists.** A room newspaper is an excellent project for sparking interest. Organize your class so that each pupil has an important contribution to make to the newspaper. For example, there will be editors, artists, staff writers. Plan with them for various sections in the paper. You may want a section on "New Books We Have Read," another on "Riddles and Jokes," and so on. This duplicated paper will also help acquaint the parents of your pupils with the learning activities in your room.

99   **Read-a-Book Special.** Design a Read-a-Book Special train. A child must read five books in order to "climb aboard" the train. A small snapshot (such as a school photo) can be pasted on the train for each child who finishes five books.

The first child to finish five books becomes the engineer. The next becomes the brakeman, and the rest become passengers. Before the year is over, chances are every child will be riding the Read-a-Book Special.

100 **Reading Notebooks.** Ask each child to keep a notebook entitled "Books I've Read" and also a 12 x 18-inch chart headed with the same title. Each child's name is written on his/her chart, and these charts are hung on one side of the room.

After a book has been read, children can answer the following questions:

1. What is the name of the book?
2. Who wrote it?
3. Name the characters in the story.
4. Which character did you like best?
5. Why did you like this character best?
6. Tell the part you liked best.

When the child has written this report in the notebook, give him/her a piece of colored construction paper, 2½" x 1¼" in size, which is folded to resemble the jacket of a book. On the outside, the child writes the name of the book and the name of the author. The number of pages in the book should be written on the inside. The child then pastes this book "jacket" to the chart.

101 **Literary Review Board.** Form a committee to read, review, and discuss new books. This group can be called the Literary Review Board. Have the board select a chairman to convene periodic meetings. In discussions, one book can be recommended to the entire school. A short review of the book can be written and read over the school's loudspeaker or printed in the school's newspaper.

102   **You've Got My Vote!**   After completing a unit of stories in basic reading texts or a book, hold an election of favorite story characters. Have children write a short "speech" that points out the positive qualities of a storybook "friend." These speeches can be delivered to the class.

Through a class vote, pare the number of nominations down to two characters. Pick a campaign manager, prepare slogans, design pins and make other preparations desired. Such slogans as "Take the right turns with Pete Burns!" or "She'll never rest— vote for Rosa Best!" will capture the interest of the class.

As a final activity, children can vote for one favorite book or story character.

103   **Class Book.**   Pupils can develop a Class Book of one-page reviews of favorite children's books. Each child can contribute a page, either through illustrations or written assignments.

The Class Book can be placed in the Reading Corner for pupils to browse through during spare moments.

104   **TV News Teams.**   Form student news teams to motivate interest in reading the newspaper.

Divide the class into eight news teams (four students in each). Assign each child a specific job within the group: anchorman, weather, sports, or local news. (Alternate jobs later on.) Carefully outline the duties of each news team member and the sources of news that will be acceptable.

This project will encourage outside reading of the news, discussion and criticism, and careful condensing and writing of news stories. The role playing will also build confidence in public speaking.

105   **First Edition.** As a class project, try to find original manuscripts, old page proofs, first editions of books, book jackets, taped interviews with authors or other interesting persons in the community, autographs of authors or any other documentation related to reading various materials. If the material cannot be brought to school, organize a trip to visit the place where the items can be found.

The children might also write to their favorite authors to request autographs. Check *Who's Who in America* for addresses, or write in care of the publishers.

106   **Special Occasions.** Holidays or special occasions can serve as times to report books read in creative ways. For instance, before Valentine's Day, let children express their love for good books. Cut a large red heart from construction paper and hang it against a white background of construction paper. In its center place a smaller white heart, with red letters saying "Books Close to Our Hearts." Each child can then cut a valentine from red or white paper, decorate it, and in the center glue a book-shape made from a rectangle of paper folded in half. The name of a favorite book goes on the "cover," with the student's name inside. This display helps to decorate the room for a valentine party.

For Halloween, construct a house full of ghosts — each representing a student who has read five books during the five-week program. Upon completion of the first book, a student receives a small paper ghost with his/her name inscribed upon it. Display it under a picture of a large-eyed black cat. When a second book is completed, the student moves his or her ghost to a colorfully decorated pumpkin. A third book finds the ghost moved to a friendly witch and the fourth to a pumpkin-witch motif. Finally, after reading a fifth book, the student can take his or her ghost to a large haunted house.

107 **Crossword Puzzles.** Have the students use their vocabulary words from a book or story to make crossword puzzles. To make certain that the children understand the format, distribute some easy crossword puzzles with answers completed. Then give each child a sheet of graph paper. You might suggest starting out by printing the longest word vertically, then fitting in the shorter words horizontally. Each student should write a question sheet and an answer sheet to accompany the puzzle. When you have checked the puzzles, return them to different students to work in their free time.

108 **Academy Awards.** Ask children to nominate their favorite book. List the ten top nominations, then allow pupils to vote for their favorite. The second, third, and fourth choices could be listed as runners-up. Have children choose a name for the award and make a poster telling about the four books.

Pupils may wish to issue a news release to be circulated among other classes in the school telling them about the award books chosen.

109 **Peace Prize.** Ask for volunteers to read and report to the class or group about the Nobel Peace Prize, which is especially interesting because its recipients have come from a variety of fields. Pupils may find the recipients listed in encyclopedias and almanacs. They can ask the school librarian to help them find further information on individual recipients. The class or group may discuss ways in which some of the work of each recipient relates to peace.

110   **Autobiographies.** Ask pupils to write autobiographies for their own enjoyment and for sharing with their classmates. A pupil with a particular interest, such as science, art, a sport, or a community activity, may concentrate on that interest in the autobiography, describing how the interest developed. Suggest that pupils keep their autobiographies to look back on and perhaps add to in a year or two. Later, they may want to write a story in which they develop or fictionalize sections of their autobiographies.

To prepare for this activity, ask students to keep journals in which they can freely express their ideas on a variety of topics. Set aside a few minutes each day for making journal entries. Remind students that continuing the journals will be helpful if they ever wish to add to their autobiographies.

111   **Meet the Characters.** Have students share their individual reading by writing a play that includes parts for their favorite characters and authors. The setting might be a book club meeting that each member of the class attends as a character or author. It might be a tropical island where selected authors and characters have been stranded. Or it might be a library where a student locked in overnight meets characters who have "come to life." Ask the students to imagine the conversation that the selected characters might have under these circumstances.

Once the class has decided on a story line, each child can write a part in which the character describes himself or herself and tells something about the book he or she appears in or has authored. When the play is performed, each child can play the part he or she has written.

112 **Story Sections.** Cut into sections a story from a children's magazine or book that is no longer usable. Distribute one section to each pupil selected. Have each pupil carefully prepare his/her section so that it can be read aloud to the class. Since the pupils have not read the story in its entirety, they will be interested in noting how the story unfolds as each pupil reads one section. Use a story that has some suspense for best results.

113 **Humpty Dumpty.** Make a chart of two-inch squares with the children's names written down the left-hand side. Draw a picture of Humpty Dumpty at the top of the chart to challenge and motivate students to "Come on up! Read and rise!" Provide some 2 × 4-inch strips of light-colored construction paper.

Each time a child reads a book, he/she will write a short book report. The child can then make a miniature book jacket by folding one of the construction paper strips in half. The child should write the title of the book on the front of the book jacket and the author's name and the date of the book report on the inside. The book jacket is then pasted to the chart to the right of the child's name.

Children who have covered all the squares opposite their names can make another book jacket to place up beside Humpty Dumpty. This final book jacket should have the child's name on the cover.

114 **Finished Products.** Several "how to" books should be included as part of the classroom library. Children can read these books and share the information gained by giving a demonstration or by displaying the finished product.

In addition, encourage the children to bring "how to" books or magazine articles from home to share with the rest of the class.

115 **Book a Trip.** "If you had a chance to take a trip, where would you go?"

This question can be posed to students to whet their interest in reading books about travel. After a travel book has been read, the student can give an illustrated lecture using postcards, photographs, slides, and pictures clipped from magazines.

The child may pretend that he/she has actually taken the trip. Added details might include the means of transportation, how long the trip took, and experiences that took place along the way. The exact locations should be identified on a map.

116 **Tell Your Author.** Have students look up information about the authors and illustrators of their favorite books in biographical reference books. Then have each student write a letter to the selected author or illustrator telling what he/she liked about the story or illustrations.

If you do not find the address of the author or illustrator, letters can be mailed in care of the publisher. Check the copyright page of the book for the publisher's address, or look it up in a reference book, such as *Literary Market Place*, at your public library.

117

Book Kite. Make a book kite with your children. As an example, draw on the board a kite with a tail and a long string. Show books recently read by the class. Then distribute small pieces of manila or construction paper and ask the children to draw pictures of major events from one of these books. These small pictures can be taped to the tail of the kite as "bows." A large picture drawn by a group of youngsters can be used as the body of the kite.

You might also build or buy a real kite and paste or tape on it a large picture of a class favorite book, drawn on tissue paper by a group of youngsters. This class kite can be flown by individual children at various times.

118

Newspaper Scrapbook. Obtain copies of newspapers and have each student keep a scrapbook containing headlines, pictures and captions, and news articles pertaining to one story. If possible, suggest major stories that might be covered from local, national, and international viewpoints. By reviewing their scrapbooks, children can follow the story as it unfolds from day to day. Suggest that students watch a TV newscast also and write a comparison of newspaper and TV coverage of the event.

To obtain enough copies of the newspaper, you might (1) ask students to bring yesterday's newspaper to school each morning; or (2) ask the local newspaper's education office for complimentary copies (enough for every member of the class).

119 Gallery and Museum Visits. If there is an art museum or gallery nearby, arrange to visit it with the class or group. The pupils can do some research beforehand by writing to the museum for information on its works of art, perhaps requesting the names of one or two artists whose important works are on exhibition. With that information, you may be able to help pupils find examples of the artists' works in art history books. Before they visit the museum, children can examine these pictures, discuss the medium or style of painting represented, and what they like or dislike about the works of art. Encourage the students to ask questions that will help them appreciate the work they see in the museum or gallery.

120 Class Anthology. Keep a class anthology during the school year. Select examples of pupils' stories, poems, compositions, and projects to include in the anthology every week.

The anthology can be arranged according to various themes, such as experiences on a class trip, poems that deal with particular subjects, and so on. A picture drawn by a pupil can be used to introduce each theme.

Try to include something by every pupil in the class or group within a few weeks. The anthology should be available for pupils to browse through.

121 Clock It. After reading a book, some pupils might enjoy planning a pantomime of a major character's activities. Suggest that they make a paper clock face with a movable hand, or write on separate pieces of paper the times mentioned in the story. One pupil can show the time and another can pantomime the actions which took place then. Other pupils could pantomime other characters in the story. Allow the pupils to show the pantomime to the class after they have practiced it.

122 **Design a Book Jacket.** Ask students to select a major theme or concept from a book and then use it to design a book jacket for the book. Locate information about the author to include in the book jacket as well as a few lines about the contents of the book. An advertisement can be prepared by individual pupils which incorporates the use of the book jacket made.

123 **Movie Script.** A popular book—or section of a book—can be selected by the class to be made into a movie. Before the movie can be made, however, a script has to be written. Ask a committee of pupils to prepare a movie script. Later, a casting director, producer, and director can be selected. Using the movie script, pupils can simulate the making of the movie based on the book chosen.

Develop a format for the script by asking the students to follow this outline:

Scene Number	Location	Characters	Action

124 **Patent Pending.** Following a study of inventors, each student imagines himself or herself a famous inventor and develops an original idea for an invention that is both practical and useful to modern society. Have the child prepare a drawing of this invention to present to the class.

Have the class vote on whether the inventor should receive a patent.

125

Books for Small Children. Allow pupils to choose from the library three or four books written for small children. Tell the pupils they should read the books quickly in order to choose books they think small children would like to hear read aloud. The students should practice reading the selected books aloud so that they can read them with fluency and good expression.

Arrange for your pupils to read to children in the lower grades. Even students with poor oral reading skills may be able to participate by choosing easy-to-read stories and reading to the youngest age group.

If it is not possible to arrange these readings, then have the pupils write reports or tell the class why they think the books they have selected would be enjoyed by young children.

Books Recommended for Children

The following list, which is not intended to be exhaustive or even comprehensive, recommends for school use fifty books that have proved to be extremely popular. Culled from a variety of sources, the list includes several books that have won Caldecott and Newberry awards.

	Author	*Title*	*Publisher*
1.	Armstrong	Sounder	Harper
2.	Baum	The Wizard of Oz	Grossett
3.	Beim	Two Is a Team	Harcourt
4.	Bemelmans	Madeline's Rescue	Houghton
5.	Bishop	The Five Chinese Brothers	Coward
6.	Brink	Caddie Woodlawn	Macmillan
7.	Butterworth	The Enormous Egg	Little
8.	Coatsworth	The Cat Who Went to Heaven	Macmillan
9.	Daugherty	Andy and the Lion	Viking
10.	D'Aulaire	Leif the Lucky	Doubleday
11.	D'Aulaire	Abraham Lincoln	Doubleday
12.	DeAngeli	Door in the Wall	Doubleday
13.	deRegniers	May I Bring a Friend?	Atheneum
14.	Edmonds	Matchlock Gun	Dodd
15.	Estes	The Hundred Dresses	Harcourt
16.	Felt	Rosa-Too-Little	Doubleday
17.	Forbes	Johnny Tremain	Houghton
18.	Gag	Millions of Cats	Coward
19.	Grahame	Wind in the Willows	Scribner

20.	Guilfoile	Nobody Listens to Andrew	Follett
21.	Hader	The Big Snow	Macmillan
22.	Hickok	Story of Helen Keller	Grossett
23.	Keats	Snowy Day	Viking
24.	Keats	Whistle for Willie	Viking
25.	Krauss	A Hole Is to Dig	Harper
26.	Krumgold	And Now Miguel	Crowell
27.	Lamorisse	The Red Balloon	Doubleday
28.	Latham	Carry On, Bowditch	Houghton
29.	Lenski	Strawberry Girl	Lippencott
30.	McClosky	Homer Price	Viking
31.	McClosky	Lentil	Viking
32.	McClosky	Make Way for Ducklings	Viking
33.	McDermott	Arrow to the Sun	Viking
34.	Milhous	Egg Tree	Scribner
35.	Milne	Winnie-the-Pooh	Dutton
36.	Parish	Amelia Bedelia	Harper
37.	Rey	Curious George	Houghton
38.	Sendak	Where the Wild Things Are	Harper
39.	Seuss	The Cat in the Hat	Random
40.	Simont	A Tree Is Nice	Harper
41.	Sperry	Call It Courage	Macmillan
42.	Stolz	A Dog on Barkham Street	Harper
43.	Tresselt, DuVoisin	White Snow, Bright Snow	Lothrop
44.	Vreekem	The Boy Who Would Not Say His Name	Follett
45.	Warner	Surprise Island	Scott, Foresman
46.	Ward	Biggest Bear	Houghton
47.	Weisgard	The Little Island	Doubleday
48.	White	Stuart Little	Harper
49.	White	Charlotte's Web	Harper
50.	Zion	Harry, the Dirty Dog	Harper

References

The following publications suggest many additional activities which will help to motivate pupils to read.

Bielawski, Joseph G., and Lawrence Pomerlean. *Reading Games Make Learning Fun.* Georgetown, Conn.: RD Communications, 1974.

Burie, Audrey Ann, and Mary Ann Heltshe. *Reading with a Smile: 90 Reading Games That Work.* Washington, D. C.: Acropolis Books, 1975.

Criscuolo, Nicholas P. *100 Individualized Activities for Reading.* Belmont, Calif.: Fearon Publishers, 1974.

————. *137 Enrichment Reading Activities.* Dansville, N. Y.: Instructor Publications, 1975.

Dorsey, Mary E. *Reading Games and Activities.* Belmont, Calif.: Fearon Publishers, 1972.

Eckgren, B. L., and Fishel V. Eckgren. *Five Hundred Live Ideas for the Grade Teacher.* Evanston, Ill.: Row, Peterson, 1952.

Garrison, Evangeline L. *Individualized Reading.* Dansville, N. Y.: Instructor Publications, 1970.

Gould, Annabelle, and Warren Schullaert. *Reading Activities for Primary and Intermediate Grades.* Dansville, N. Y.: Instructor Publications, 1972.

Heyman, Marjorie Howe. *Enriching Your Reading Program.* Belmont, Calif.: Fearon Publishers, 1972.

Mallett, Jerry J. *Classroom Reading Games Activities Kit.* New York: Center for Applied Research, 1975.

Meuser, Anne Marie. *Reading Aids Through the Grades.* New York: Teachers College Press, 1975.

Mulac, Margaret. *Fun and Games.* New York: Harper & Row, 1956.

Spache, Evelyn. *Reading Activities for Child Involvement.* Rockleigh, N. J.: Allyn and Bacon, 1972.

Thompson, Richard A. *Energizers for Reading Instruction.* West Nyack, N. Y.: Parker Publishing, 1973.

Wagner, Guy, and Max Hosier. *Reading Games.* Darien, Conn.: Teachers Publishing, 1972.

Idea Books That Free You to Teach

*Here are more selected Reading and Language Arts titles
from Fearon Pitman's high-motivation Teacher-Aid line.
And every year we add exciting new books. Watch for them!*

READING GAMES & ACTIVITIES; Dorsey. 7″ × 10″; 128 pp., illus. For primary & intermediate grades, games to develop visual & auditory perception of rhyme, consonants, long & short vowels, consonant blends, vocabulary. #5810-1.

20 READING COMPREHENSION GAMES; Love. 8-1/2″ × 11″; 88 pp., MAKEMASTER ® worksheets. Lively duplicatable games in six major skill areas encourage student involvement & progress. Great graphics! #5800-4.

100 INDIVIDUALIZED ACTIVITIES FOR READING; Criscuolo. 5-1/2″ × 8-1/4″; 64 pp., illus. For primary and intermediate students, a battery of reading helps: motivation, auditory & visual exercises, word & vocabulary analysis, comprehension activities. #5065-8.

READING SKILLS: Simple Games, Aids, Devices to Stimulate Reading; Kingsley. 7″ × 10″; 32 pp., illus. Suggestions to involve elementary children in word analysis, phonics, word recognition, and other skills, as a basis for reading success. #5825-X.

77 GAMES FOR READING GROUPS; Metzner. 6″ × 9″; 56 pp. Games build word recognition, word analysis, vocabulary, and other skills basic to reading. Largely self-managing, for independent group work! Elementary grades. #6371-7.

BIRDSEYE VIEW OF LANGUAGE ARTS: Worksheets in Spelling & Phonics, Word Structure, Word Meaning, Grammar & Usage; Cory. 8-1/2″ × 11″; 224 pp. Exciting mini-stories, puzzles, word games & codes on duplicatable MAKEMASTER ® worksheets give intermediate students a humorous new approach to practice in basic language skills. A treasure-trove. #0701-9.

HANDS-ON GRAMMAR: An Instant Resource; Laird. 5-1/2″ × 8-1/2″; 48 pp. An instant access list of grammatical definitions with examples for teachers, students, writers, executives—ANYONE who needs to know! #3072-0.

IDEAS FOR LEARNING CENTERS: Discovery Learning for Children; Moore & Greenlee. 8-1/2″ × 11″; 128 pp., 2 c. illus., spiral bound. For the intermediate student, self-directed, self-rewarding learning with a major focus in language arts. Wide range of topics, structured to build essential skills. #3840-2.

For a complete Teacher-Aid catalog, write to **Pitman Learning, Inc.**
6 Davis Drive, Belmont, California 94002. Or telephone (415) 592-7810.